BASKETBALL

BASKETBALL: RULES OF THE GAME

BRYANT LLOYD

The Rourke Book Co., Inc.
Vero Beach, Florida 32964

PHOTO CREDITS
cover, p. 6, 10, 13, 18 © Bryant Lloyd; p. 9, 12, 15, 16, 22 © Andrew Young; p. 7, 19, 20 courtesy Beacon News, Aurora, IL

EDITORIAL SERVICES:
Penworthy Learning Systems

Library of Congress Cataloging-in-Publication Data

Lloyd, Bryant. 1942-
    Basketball: rules of the game / by Bryant Lloyd.
        p. cm. — (Basketball)
    Includes index
    Summary: Provides a simple introduction to the game of basketball, covering layout of the court, rules of play, scoring, and terminology.
    ISBN 1-55916-228-7
    1. Basketball—Rules—Juvenile literature. [1. Basketball.]
I. Title II. Series: Lloyd, Bryant, 1942- Basketball.
GV885.45.L56 1997
796.323'02'022—dc21   97–8437
                                                            CIP
                                                            AC

Printed in the USA

TABLE OF CONTENTS

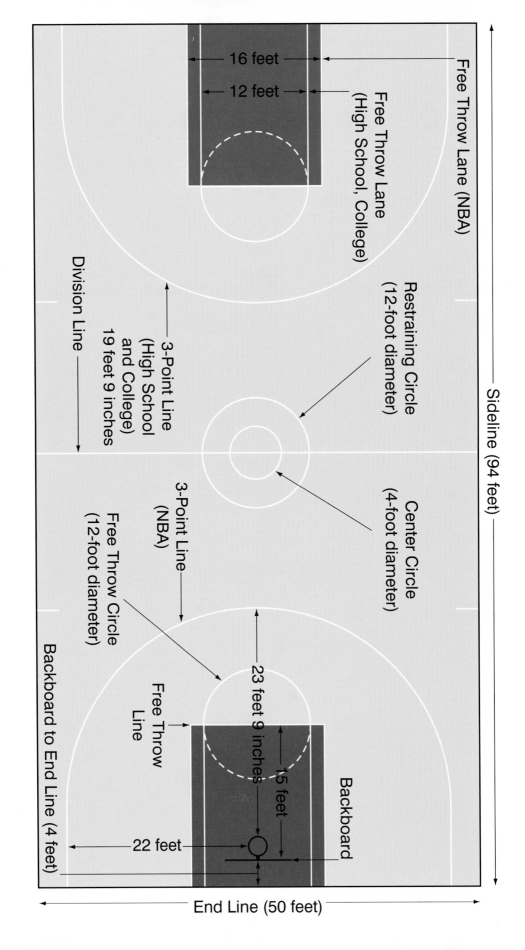

THE COURT

Basketball games are played on a flat surface called a court or floor. The court is a rectangle shape. It usually has a wood surface.

A **regulation** (REG yuh LAY shun) court is 94 feet (29 meters) long and 50 feet (15 meters) wide. High school courts may be 10 feet (3 meters) shorter in length.

A basket attached to a backboard is mounted at each end of the court. The rim of each basket is 10 feet above the floor.

Basketball is an international sport, and games between nations are played by international rules. International rules include a 30-second shot clock but are similar to American rules in other ways. In other words, the offense has 30 seconds in which to take a shot.

Diagram of court

TEAMS

A regulation basketball game is played between two teams. Each team has five players on the court at one time.

Each team works together as a unit. A team is sometimes trying to score. At other times, it is trying to stop its opponent from scoring.

A maplewood floor—the "hard court"—is the setting for this middle school practice.

By grabbing a rebound off the other team's backboard, a player (yellow uniform) puts his team on the offensive.

The team with the ball is the team on **offense** (AW fents). It it the team "attacking" the basket. The team trying to prevent a basket is the **defense** (DEE fents).

After a team scores, the other team is awarded the ball.

THE CLOCK

A regulation basketball game, like football or hockey, is played for a fixed time. High schools play four 8-minute quarters. Colleges play two 20-minute halves. The National Basketball Association (NBA) plays four 12-minute quarters. Junior high and grade school teams play shorter quarters than high school.

The clock stops when a **foul** (FOWL) is committed, whenever the ball goes out of bounds, and after rules are broken. The clock also stops for time-outs and certain injuries.

The clock is run by an **official** (uh FISH ul), one of the people who manage the playing of the game.

An official game clock is started and stopped by an official timekeeper. Time-outs, free-throws, and turnovers are reasons to stop the clock.

4:52
HOME
BONUS
POSS.
VISITOR
26
4
19
FOULS
PLAYER
FOUL
FOULS
4
45
2
2
GAME
WINS

STARTING THE GAME

A regulation basketball game begins with a center jump, or jump ball. A circle at the center of the court marks the jump spot.

Two players stand inside the circle. These players are usually the tallest players on each team.

An official throws the ball up between the two players in the center circle. Both players jump and try to swat the ball to one of their teammates standing outside the circle.

Violations result in the loss of possession of the basketball. Common violations include a double dribble, two hands on the ball during a dribble, three seconds in the free-throw lane, and traveling. Traveling occurs when a player takes steps while holding the ball.

A basketball game begins with a jump ball in the circle at center court.

MOVING THE BALL

One player grabs the swatted ball from the center jump. That player's team then has **possession** (puh ZESH un)—ownership—of the ball. That team is now on offense and will try to make a basket.

A team moves the ball around by dribbling or passing.

A player dribbles the ball as he walks or runs on the court.

The team with the ball can move it by passing or dribbling. Dribbling means bouncing the ball with one hand. A player with the ball cannot carry it. It must be dribbled or passed. Meanwhile, players on defense cannot touch the player who is dribbling or passing the ball.

FIELD GOALS

Basketball teams score points by tossing the ball through the basket at "their" end of the court. Usually, teams try to work the ball as close to the basket as they can before shooting.

Shots that go into the baskets are goals, or field goals. Most goals count two points.

Baskets from beyond the arc count three points. The arc, or three-point line, in college and high school is 19 feet, 9 inches (6 meters) from the backboard. The National Basketball Association (NBA) line is 22 feet (over 6 meters) away.

A player who is called for five fouls in high school or college is disqualified from the remainder of the game. NBA players are disqualified after their sixth foul.

A player attempts a two-point field goal. A shot from beyond 19 feet, 9 inches (6 meters) is a three-point goal in high school and college games.

REBOUNDS

More shots miss the basket than go into it. Most missed shots bounce off the rim or backboard.

A missed shot that bounces into the field of play is a **rebound** (REE BOUND). Players on both teams are free to grab a rebound. Whichever team takes the rebound becomes the offensive team.

Sometimes a missed shot, without being touched, bounces out of bounds. Then the ball is awarded to the team that had been on defense.

A team that goes onto offense has 10-seconds to bring the ball across the half-court line.

Players battle for a rebound, which is a missed shot bouncing toward the floor.

FOULS

The flow of a basketball game may be stopped by a foul. A foul is a **violation** (vy uh LAY shun) of basketball rules. An official blows a whistle to call a foul.

A personal foul may be called for a push, slap, bump, hold, block, charge or other contact that is against the rules.

The player on the right has fouled the ball handler by grabbing his right hand.

The player on the right will receive a foul if she touches the player with the ball.

A foul often gives the fouled player a chance to shoot a foul shot, or free throw. A free throw is shot from a line 15 feet (about 4 1/2 meters) from the backboard. Each basket from the free throw line counts one point.

VIOLATIONS

Other violations, like fouls, result when rules of the game are broken, usually by the offense. A violation turns the ball over to the team that had been on defense.

The shot clock violation is common in college and professional basketball. An NBA team must shoot within 24 seconds. College men have 45 seconds to shoot. College women have 30 seconds. High school players do not have a shot clock.

More than 750 college teams play in the three divisions of the NCAA (National Collegiate Athletic Association). Another 500 play in the NAIA (National Association of Intercollegiate Athletics).

Tightly guarded, the player with the ball (yellow uniform) has five seconds to shoot, pass, or dribble. If he cannot do one or the other, the ball will go to the defense (white uniforms).

Glossary

defense (DEE fents) — the team that is defending its basket

foul (FOWL) — any type of physical contact not allowed by basketball rules and that results in a game official stopping play

offense (AW fents) — the team that is trying to score

official (uh FISH ul) — any one of several people who manage the time and activity of a regulation basketball game

possession (puh ZESH un) — to have the ball; ownership

rebound (REE BOUND) — a missed shot that hits the rim or backboard and bounces into the field of play in a basketball game

regulation (REG yuh LAY shun) — refers to a contest or equipment that is set up or made according to exact rules of the game

violation (vy uh LAY shun) — the breaking of a rule of the game, especially by the offense

A player "keeps" a dribble only as long as he or she continues to bounce the ball

INDEX